Mapping Our World

Australia
and the
South Pacific

by
Fran Sammis

Benchmark Books

MARSHALL CAVENDISH
NEW YORK

Marshall Cavendish Corporation
99 White Plains Road
Tarrytown, New York 10591-9001

© Marshall Cavendish Corporation 2000

Series created by Blackbirch Graphics, Inc.

Photo Credits
Page 14: ©Chuck Szymanski/International Stock; pages 15 and 25: ©Peter Krinninger/International Stock; page 19: ©Gerard Lacz/Peter Arnold; page 39: North Wind Picture Archives; page 40: The Library of Congress; page 53: ©Michael Ventura/International Stock; page 56: ©Chad Ehlers/International Stock; page 57: ©Buddy Mays/International Stock; page 59: ©Orion/International Stock.

Printed in Hong Kong

Library of Congress Cataloging-in-Publication Data

Sammis, Fran
    Australia and the South Pacific / by Fran Sammis
       p.   cm. — (Mapping our world)
    Includes bibliographical references and index.
    Summary: Text, photographs, and maps introduce information about the climate, land use, resources, plants and animals, population, politics, and religions of Australia, New Zealand, and the islands of the South Pacific.
    ISBN 0-7614-0373-6
    1. Cartography—Australia—Juvenile literature. 2. Cartography—New Zealand—Juvenile literature. 3. Cartography—Oceania—Juvenile literature. [1. Cartography—Australia. 2. Cartography—New Zealand. 3. Cartography—Oceania. 4. Australia—Maps. 5. New Zealand—Maps. 6. Oceania—Maps.] I. Title. II. Series: Sammis, Fran. Mapping our world.
  GA1681.S23   2000
  912—dc21

98-27958
CIP
AC

Contents

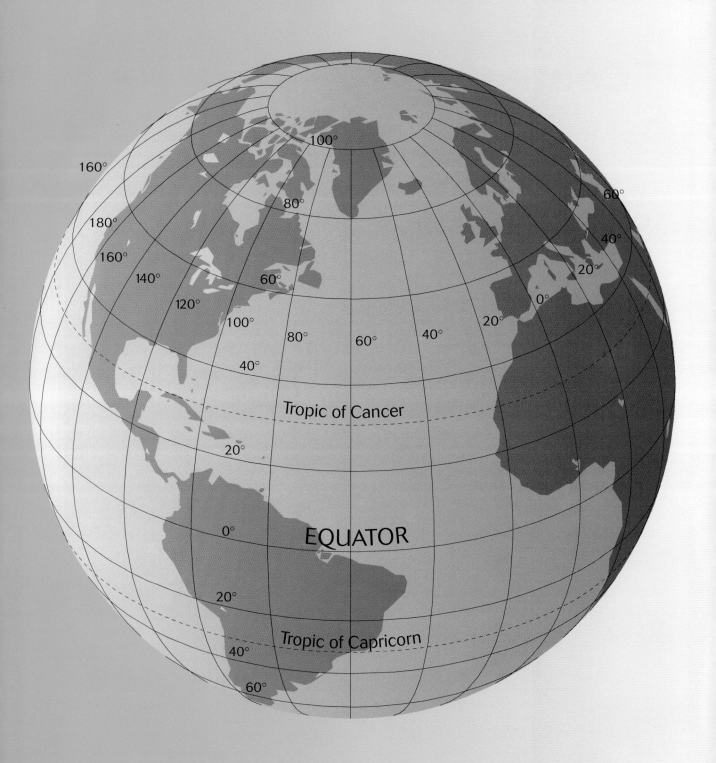

160°
180°
160°
140°
120°
100°
80°
60°
40°
100°
80°
60°
40°
20°
0°
20°
40°
60°
20°
0°
20°
Tropic of Cancer
EQUATOR
20°
Tropic of Capricorn
40°
60°

4

The Importance of Maps

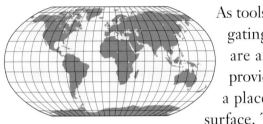

As tools for understanding and navigating the world around us, maps are an essential resource. Maps provide us with a representation of a place, drawn or printed on a flat surface. The place that is shown may be as vast as the solar system or as small as a neighborhood park. What we learn about the place depends on the kind of map we are using.

Kinds of Maps

Physical maps show what the land itself looks like. These maps can be used to locate and identify natural geographic features such as mountains, bodies of water, deserts, and forests.

Distribution maps show where something can be found. There are two kinds of distribution maps. One shows the range or area a feature covers, such as a map showing where grizzly bears live or where hardwood forests grow.

The second kind of distribution map shows the density of a feature. That is, how much or how little of the feature is present. These maps allow us to see patterns in the way a feature is distributed. Rainfall and population maps are two examples of this kind of distribution map.

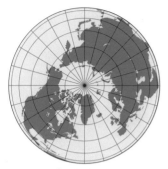

Globular

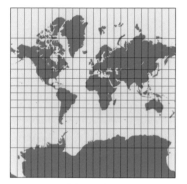

Mercator

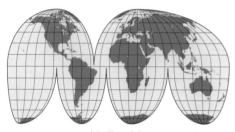

Mollweide

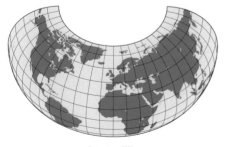

Armadillo

Political maps show us how an area is divided into countries, states, provinces, or other units. They also show where cities and towns are located. Major highways and transportation routes are also included on some kinds of political maps.

Movement maps help us find our way around. They can be road maps, street maps, and public transportation maps. Special movement maps called "charts" are used by airplane or boat pilots to navigate through air or on water.

Why Maps Are Important

Many people depend on maps to do their jobs. A geologist, for example, uses maps of Earth's structure to locate natural resources such as coal or petroleum. A transportation planner will use population maps to determine where new roads may need to be built.

A map can tell us how big a place is, where one place is in relation to another, what a place was like in the past, and what it's like now. Maps help us understand and move through our own part of the world and the rest of the world, too. Some maps even help us move through our solar system and universe!

Terms to Know

Maps are created and designed by incorporating many different elements and accepted cartographic (mapmaking) techniques. Often, maps showing the exact same area will differ from one another, depending upon the choice or critical elements, such as scale and projection. Following is a brief listing of some key mapmaking terms.

Projection. A projection is a way to represent the round Earth on a flat surface. There are a number of different ways to project, or transfer, round-Earth information to a flat surface, though each method results in some distortion. That is, areas may appear larger or smaller than they really are—or closer or farther apart. The maps on page 6 show a few varieties of projections.

Latitude. Lines of latitude, or parallels, run parallel to the equator (the imaginary center of Earth's circumference) and are used to locate points north and south of the equator. The equator is 0 degrees latitude, the north pole is 90 degrees north latitude, and the south pole is 90 degrees south latitude.

Longitude. Lines of longitude, or meridians, run at right angles to the equator and meet at the north and south poles. Lines of longitude are used to locate points east and west of the prime meridian.

Prime meridian. An imaginary line that runs through Greenwich, England; considered 0 degrees longitude. Lines to the west of the prime meridian go halfway around the world to 180 degrees west longitude; lines to the east go to 180 degrees east longitude.

Hemisphere. A half circle. Dividing the world in half from pole to pole along the prime meridian gives you the eastern and western hemispheres. Dividing the world in half at the equator gives you the northern and southern hemispheres.

Scale. The relationship of distance on a map to the actual distance on the ground. Scale can be expressed in three ways:

1. As a ratio—1:63,360 (one inch equals 63,360 inches)
2. Verbally—one inch equals one mile
3. Graphically— [1 mi.   ]

Because 63,360 inches equal one mile, these scales give the same information: one map-inch equals one mile on the ground.

Large-scale maps show a small area, such as a city park, in great detail. Small-scale maps show a large area, such as an entire continent, in much less detail, and on a much smaller scale.

The Art and Process of Mapmaking

Maps have been made for thousands of years. Early maps, based on first-hand exploration, were some of the most accurate tools of their

◀◀ *Opposite: The maps shown here are just four of the many different projections in which the world can be displayed.*

225 million years ago

1

180 million years ago

2

65 million years ago

3

present day

4

time. Others, based on guesses about what an area was like, were often very beautiful, but were not especially accurate.

As technology—such as photography and flight—evolved, cartographers (mapmakers) were able not only to map most of Earth in detail, they were also able to make maps of our solar system.

To make a map today, cartographers first determine what a map is to show and who is most likely to use it. Then, they assemble the information they will need for the map, which can come from many different kinds of experts—such as meteorologists, geologists, and surveyors—as well as from aerial photography or satellite feedback.

Mapping a Changing Earth

If you traced around all the land masses shown on a world map, then cut them out and put them together like a jigsaw puzzle, the result would look something like map 1 at the top of this page. Scientists think this is how Earth looked about 225 million years ago.

Over time, this single continent, Pangaea (Pan–JEE–uh), slowly broke apart into two land masses called Laurasia and Gondwanaland (map 2). Maps 3 and 4 show how the land masses continued to break up and drift apart over millions of years, until the continents assumed the shapes and positions we recognize today. Earth has not, however, finished changing.

Scientists have established that Earth's surface is made up of sections called tectonic plates. These rigid plates, shown in the map on page 9, are in

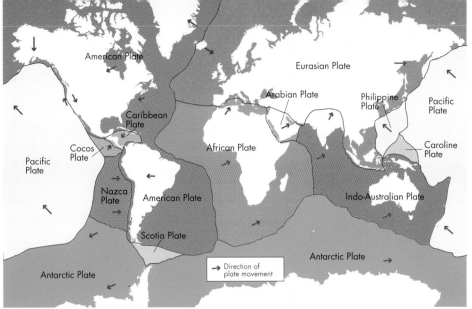

◀ **Left:** *The tectonic plates that lie beneath Earth's surface are in a slow but constant motion.*

◀◀ **Opposite:** *The continents of our planet were once clumped together but have spread apart over millions of years in what is called continental drift.*

slow, constant motion, moving from 1/4 to 1 inch a year. As they move, they take the continents and sea floors with them. Sometimes, their movements cause disasters, such as earthquakes and volcanic activity.

After many more millions of years have passed, our Earth's continents will again look very different from what we know today.

Reading a Map

In order for a map to be useful, it must be the right kind of map for the job. A small-scale map of Illinois would not help you find your way around Chicago; for that, you would need a large-scale map of the city. A physical map of North America would not tell you where most of the people live; you would need a distribution map that shows population.

Once you have found the right map, you will need to refer to the map legend, or key, to be sure you are interpreting the map's information correctly. Depending on the type of map, the legend tells the scale used for the map, and notes the meaning of any symbols and colors used.

In their most basic form, maps function as place finders. They show us where places are, and we use these maps to keep from getting lost. But as you have begun to see, maps can tell us much more about our world than simply where places are located. Just how much more, you'll discover in the chapters ahead.

PAPUA NEW GUINEA

SOLOMON
ISLANDS

Arafura Sea

Timor Sea

Gulf of
Carpentaria

Cape
York
Peninsula

Coral Sea

VANUATU

FIJI

NEW CALEDONIA

WESTERN
PLATEAU

CENTRAL LOWLANDS

EASTERN HIGHLANDS

AUSTRALIA

Pacific
Ocean

Lake
Eyre

Darling River

Great Australian Bight

Spencer Gulf

Murray River

Australian Alps

Mt. Kosciusko

Indian
Ocean

Bass
Strait

Tasman Sea

NORTH
ISLAND

NEW ZEALAND

Southern
Alps

Mt. Cook

Tasmania

Sutherland
Falls

SOUTH
ISLAND

STEWART
ISLAND

Physical Map

Key

*Feet (meters)
above sea level*

- 20 (6)
- 1,000 (305)
- 5,000 (1,524)
- 10,000 (3,048)

Mapping Natural Zones and Regions

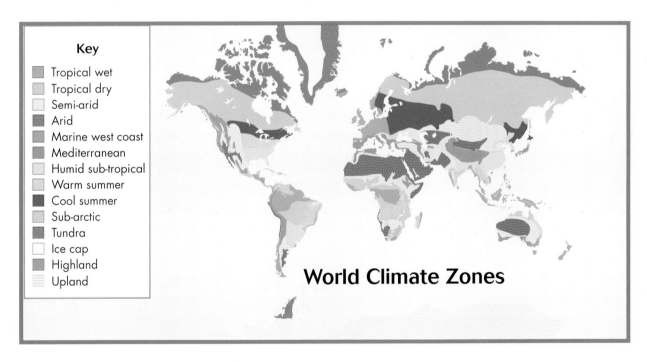

Key

- Tropical wet
- Tropical dry
- Semi-arid
- Arid
- Marine west coast
- Mediterranean
- Humid sub-tropical
- Warm summer
- Cool summer
- Sub-arctic
- Tundra
- Ice cap
- Highland
- Upland

World Climate Zones

Australia is the world's smallest continent and the only one that is occupied by a single country. With an area of about 2,969,000 square miles (7,689,710 square kilometers), Australia is slightly smaller than the continental United States.

Two islands make up Australia: the main island and the island state of Tasmania, to the south. The greatest north-south distance on

▲ *Above: Australia and North Africa have similar climates.*

◄◄ *Opposite: As you can see from this map, Australia is relatively flat.*

the mainland is approximately 1,950 miles (3,138 kilometers). The greatest east-west distance is about 2,500 miles (4,023 kilometers). The Indian Ocean borders Australia on the west and south; the Pacific Ocean borders it on the east.

Australia lies about 2,000 miles (3,219 kilometers) southeast of mainland Asia, just below the island of New Guinea. Papua New Guinea, the eastern half of the island, is considered a South Pacific nation. The western half belongs to Indonesia and is considered part of Asia. It is covered in the volume of Mapping Our World called *Asia*. At a distance of about 100 miles (161 kilometers), Papua New Guinea is Australia's nearest neighboring country. New Calendonia, a French territory, lies about 1,000 miles (1,609 kilometers) to the southeast.

Take a look at any of the maps in this volume. New Zealand seems to be close to Australia, which lies across the Tasman Sea. However, New Zealand is 1,200 miles (1,931 kilometers) away—about the distance from New York to Minneapolis, Minnesota.

To learn about what Australia and the South Pacific are like, you might start by referring to maps that show their physical features (topography), climate, land use, and other natural characteristics. The islands shown on these maps and discussed in this volume are among the largest in the South Pacific. But they are not the only ones. There are thousands more scattered throughout that vast area. However, it would take a very small-scale map to include all the islands of the South Pacific. And at that scale, it would be difficult to show any meaningful, specific information about the topics covered here.

The Topography of Australia

Australia is the flattest of the world's continents. It can be divided into three main regions: the Eastern Highlands, the Central Lowlands, and the Western Plateau.

The highest elevations are found in the Eastern Highlands, a region that follows the coastline from Cape York Peninsula in the northeast to Melbourne in the southeast. Tasmania is also a part of the Highlands. Underneath the Bass Strait, which divides Tasmania from the mainland, lies the connecting section of the Highlands that sank thousands of years ago.

The Eastern Highlands region is a mixture of low mountains, high plateaus, and hills. The southern part of the Highlands is the most mountainous. This area is called the Australian Alps, though it is not nearly as high or rugged as the Alps of Europe. Mount Kosciusko, Australia's highest point at 7,310 feet (2,228 meters) above sea level, is located here. It is less than half the height of Mont Blanc, the tallest mountain in Europe. (Mont Blanc is in France.)

The Highlands are also called the Great Dividing Range because they divide the way the rivers flow. Rivers flow directly to the ocean if they begin on the eastern side of the range, and they wander through the Central Lowlands if they begin on the western side.

Australia's main river system originates in the Highlands. It consists of the Murray River and its tributaries—the Darling, Lachlan, and Murrumbidgee Rivers. The Darling is Australia's longest river at 1,702 miles (2,739 kilometers), but the Murray is more important because at 1,609 miles (2,589 kilometers), it is the longest river that flows year-round. Most of Australia's rivers, including the Darling, are dry for at least part of the year.

Immediately west of the Eastern Highlands is the Central Lowlands region. This basically flat area extends roughly from the Gulf of Carpentaria in the north to Spencer Gulf in the south. As the name suggests, the Lowlands is where you'll find the lowest areas on the continent. Australia's lowest point, Lake Eyre, is 52 feet (16 meters) below sea level—when it's there at all! Most of the country's lakes are dry for long stretches, often years at a time. Lake Eyre is thought to have completely filled only two or three times during its existence.

In the central part of the Lowlands is the Simpson Desert—one of Australia's four main deserts. The other three—the Great Sandy, Gibson, and Great Victoria Deserts—are in the center of the Western Plateau region, which covers the western two-thirds of the continent.

As you can see on the physical map, the Western Plateau is nearly as flat as the Central Lowlands region, with the exception of a few low mountain ranges. At the center of the continent is Ayers Rock, or Iluṟu in Aboriginal. This immense, flat-topped rock is 6 miles (10 kilometers) around and 1,000 feet (305 meters) tall. It is the largest monolith (huge stone) in the world and a major tourist attraction.

The Topography of New Zealand and Other South Pacific Islands

In contrast to the vast, flat expanses of Australia, New Zealand's topography is compact and mountainous. No point in New Zealand is more than 70 miles (113 kilometers) from the sea.

The two largest islands that make up New Zealand are South Island and North Island. Tiny Stewart Island is the southernmost part of the country. On South Island, the Southern Alps run almost the full length of the west coast. Here you'll find New Zealand's highest point, 12,283-foot (3,744-meter) Mount Cook. Fjords (narrow sea

▼ *Below:* The majestic Mount Cook is the highest point in New Zealand.

▲ **Above:** *The mountains of Papua New Guinea are as tall as the Alps in Europe.*

channels between steep mountain walls) cut into the southwest coast, and rolling plains line the east coast. Sutherland Falls, the world's fourth-highest waterfall at 1,904 feet (580 meters) is on South Island.

On North Island, extinct and active volcanic mountains fan across the center of the island. Geysers shoot hot water high in the air, and boiling mud pools ooze and bubble. A quieter landscape is found in the lowland hills and plains that make up the northern peninsula and the eastern and southern coasts of North Island.

The rugged mountains that cover Papua New Guinea's interior are broken in places by high plateaus and deep valleys. Mount Wilhelm, the country's highest mountain, at 14,793 feet (4,509 meters), is twice as tall as Australia's highest point. Lowlands lie along the north and south coasts of the island, with swampy deltas at the mouths of the Fly and Sepik Rivers.

The other islands in the South Pacific are generally classified as either high or low islands. High islands are hilly or mountainous. Some, such as the islands of Fiji, were formed by volcanic activity, and they are made up mostly of volcanic rock. Others, such as Papua New Guinea, may have active volcanoes on them, but they were not formed by volcanic activity.

The low islands, called "atolls," are made of coral sand and have a coral reef nearby. Each island, or group of islands, and its reef form a circle around a shallow body of water called a lagoon. Atolls usually are no more than 30 feet (9 meters) high at their tallest point; some are as little as 5 feet (7.5 meters) high. The Tuamoto Islands, which are in the middle of the Pacific Ocean, are atolls. (They do not appear on maps in this volume.)

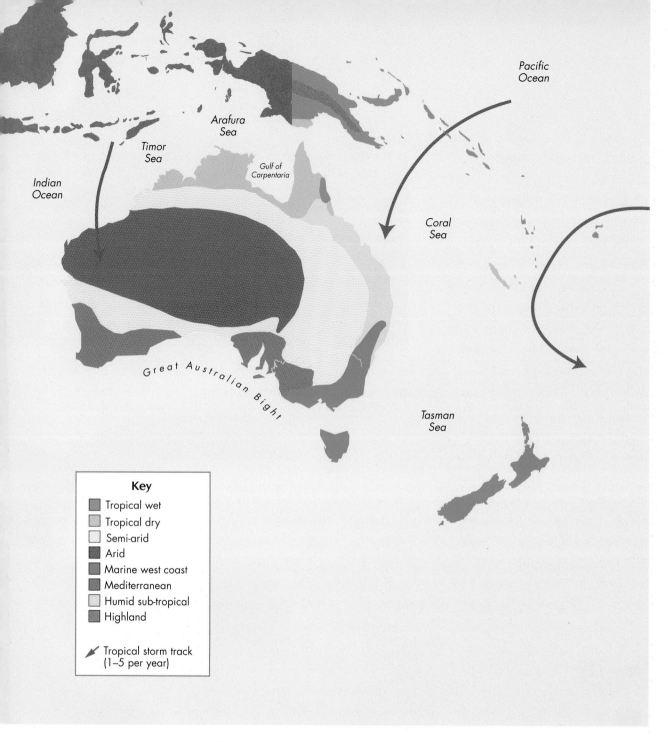

Pacific Ocean

Arafura Sea

Timor Sea

Indian Ocean

Gulf of Carpentaria

Coral Sea

Great Australian Bight

Tasman Sea

Key

- Tropical wet
- Tropical dry
- Semi-arid
- Arid
- Marine west coast
- Mediterranean
- Humid sub-tropical
- Highland

Tropical storm track
(1–5 per year)

▲ *Above: Most of Australia is either arid or semi-arid.*

Climate and Weather

The physical traits of Australia and the South Pacific are affected by their climate. Climate and weather are not the same thing. Weather is short-lived; it changes from day to day. Climate is the average characteristics of the weather in a given place over a long period of time. Although climates can change, they do so much more slowly than weather—over many years, rather than days.

Meteorologists use a variety of high-tech methods to gather the information that allows them to analyze and predict the weather. Among those methods are sophisticated ways of viewing and mapping the world.

Analyzing and Predicting Weather

The major elements that are used to describe the weather and categorize climate are: temperature, precipitation, humidity, amount of sunshine, wind, and air pressure.

Manned and unmanned weather stations on land and at sea, weather balloons, airplanes, and satellites are all used in gathering weather information for analysis. Radar, cameras, and thermal infrared sensors monitor and record the weather conditions.

The information from these sources is sent to weather centers throughout the world by means of a worldwide satellite system called the Global Telecommunications System (GTS). The information is fed into computers that record and analyze the data, which can then be compiled into highly detailed and informative maps. The GTS also allows weather centers to share their data.

By studying global weather patterns over a long time, climatologists can map climatic regions—areas that have similar climates. The world climate zones map on page 11 is just one example of this kind of map.

The Climate of Australia

Of the countries included on the map on page 16, Australia has the most distinctly varied climate, ranging from mild (marine west coast) to hot and dry (arid).

- A tropical dry climate, indicated in green on the map, is typical of the north coast sections of Australia. This area is hot, and has both wet and dry seasons. In the wet season—from November through April—rainfall is heavy, and violent storms are not uncommon.

- The humid sub-tropical area of Australia's east coast is marked by warm to hot summers, mild winters, and moderate, year-round rainfall.
- The southeast coast of the mainland and the island of Tasmania have a marine west coast climate. This mild climate, colored blue-green on the map, features warm summers, cool winters, and moderate precipitation throughout the year. The only areas of Australia that have snow are located in this climate region. In the winter, snow falls in the Australian Alps and the mountains of Tasmania.
- The southwest coast and, to the east, the area around Adelaide have a Mediterranean climate, colored deep blue. Here the summers are hot and dry, and the winters are mild and rainy.
- The majority of Australia has a dry climate, with varying precipitation. The semi-arid areas (colored gold) receive between 10 and 20 inches (25 and 51 centimeters) of rain a year. The arid desert areas (colored red), receive even less—usually under 10 inches a year. Summer daytime temperatures in the deserts average over 85 degrees Fahrenheit (29 degrees Celsius), and often go to 110 degrees Fahrenheit (43 degrees Celsius) or higher.

The rainy season occurs during the summer in the north and the winter in the south. Australia's summer is December through February, and winter is June through August.

The Climate of New Zealand and Other Islands

Overall, New Zealand's climate is moist and mild, much like southeastern Australia's climate. The west coast of New Zealand is the wettest part of the country, averaging about 100 inches (254 centimeters) of rain a year. At Milford Sound, in the southwest corner of South Island, the average annual rainfall is 240 inches (610 centimeters). Snow falls mainly in the mountains.

Most other islands of the South Pacific have a tropical wet climate. They are hot and rainy all year. Papua New Guinea and Fiji are two such island groups, as you can see on the map on page 16. New Caledonia, however, has a tropical dry climate. It is hot there all year, with wet and dry seasons. In general, high islands, such as Fiji and Papua New Guinea, receive more rain than low islands.

Animals

Early explorers of Australia found many animals they had never encountered before. Among the wildlife they described were kangaroos and black swans. Many familiar animals were found living in Australia, too, of course. But, even today, the continent is known for its unusual animals.

The most unusual Australian mammals are the platypus and the echidna, or spiny anteater. Unlike other mammals that give birth to live young, the platypus and echidna lay eggs. A platypus has a duck-like bill, otter-like feet, and a beaver-like tail. It lives near streams and rivers, primarily in eastern Australia. Echidnas, which have long snouts and are almost completely covered in sharp spines, are found throughout most of Australia.

Almost half the mammals in Australia are marsupials. These are animals that carry their young in pouches. Among the most famous are kangaroos, which live everywhere but the driest deserts. There are more than 40 species of kangaroos living in Australia, ranging in size from 9 feet (3 meters) long, including the tail, to less than 1 foot (0.3 meter) long. One species, which looks rather like a small bear with a long tail, lives in trees.

Another of Australia's well-known marsupial is the sleepy, slow-moving koala. Because koalas eat only one kind of eucalyptus tree leaf, they are found only in the coastal areas where that particular tree grows.

▼ *Below: The platypus is one of Australia's most unusual animals.*

New Zealand's only native mammals are bats; all other mammals were brought in from other countries. There are no snakes in New Zealand, but there are other reptiles, including the rare tuatara, an iguana-like lizard that lives on New Zealand's coastal islands. This lizard is the last surviving member of a family of reptiles that lived more than 100 million years ago. The tuatara grows to about 2.5 feet (0.8 meter) long and can live to be 300 years old.

The deserts in central Australia are home to a wide variety of animals, most of which live in underground burrows to escape the daytime heat. Snakes slither across the sand while scorpions scuttle by, looking for prey. Long-tongued lizards search out insects, and eagles and buzzards soar overhead, keeping a sharp eye out for their next meal.

Birds are so common in Australia that on one old map, it is labeled *Terra psittacorum*, which means "Land of Parrots" in Latin. The black swans that so amazed the early European explorers are native only to Australia. Lyrebirds, which have long and beautiful tail feathers, fill the air with their songs, while the crow-sized kookaburra adds its strange "laugh." In addition, more than 50 species of parrots—both small and large—fill the Australian landscape with bright flashes of color.

Two flightless birds live in Australia. The emu, which is about the size of an ostrich, and the smaller cassowary. Like the ostrich, both birds depend on their strong legs to carry them from place to place. Cassowaries live in the tropical rain forests of Queensland's northeast coast, as well as in Papua New Guinea. Emus live on the dry plains of Australia's outback.

New Zealand is also known for the number of flightless birds that are found there. The most well known is the kiwi, New Zealand's unofficial symbol. This round, rooster-sized, hairy-looking bird lives in the mountain forests, where it is active at night.

In addition to the many unusual animals that inhabit the land, thousands more find a home in and around Australia's Great Barrier Reef. Located off Queensland's coast, the Great Barrier Reef is the largest coral reef system in the world. About 400 species of coral, 1,500 species of fish, and 4,000 species of shellfish make their home here. Turtles, dolphins, and dugong—a relative of the manatee—also inhabit these waters.

Outside of Australia and New Zealand, animal life is most varied in Papua New Guinea, where snakes, crocodiles, tree kangaroos, anteaters, mice and rats, birds, and butterflies all make their home. Land crabs and lizards scuttle across the drier islands. Millions of shearwaters—large, web-footed birds—skim the waters surrounding many of the islands of the South Pacific.

Plants

Brilliantly colored flowers are found in the wetter areas of Australia and in the desert. There, the seeds lie dormant until a heavy rainfall brings them to life, sometimes for only a few days each year. New Zealand has many ferns, mosses, and vines, but few flowering plants.

The two most common Australian plants are the acacias and eucalyptuses—Australians refer to them as "wattles" and "eucalypts." There are hundreds of species of each plant, but the majority of Australia's trees—three out of every four—are eucalyptuses. These trees are valuable for timber and a fragrant oil they produce. One kind of eucalyptus tree provides a home for the koala—and its only source of food.

Where rainfall is plentiful, both acacias and eucalyptuses grow into tall trees. Short tree and shrub species have adapted to the drier areas, where there is also scrub grass growing. A shrub called "salt-bush," because of its salty leaves, grows throughout the dry grazing land, providing feed for sheep and cattle.

Evergreen trees and fern trees make up most of the forests of New Zealand, and dense forests or jungles are found on some of the high islands, such as Papua New Guinea. Low islands with little rainfall are covered mainly in grass or low shrubs. Palm trees and a wide variety of flowering plants are found on low islands that get more rain.

How Climate and Topography Affect People

As we have seen, climate greatly affects plant and animal life. Of course, a region's climate and topography can affect many aspects of human life as well. Among them:

Population distribution. More people tend to settle in areas that have a mild or moderate climate, adequate rainfall, and fairly level, open land. Population will be less densely distributed in regions that are mountainous or thickly forested, and in regions with climates that are very cold or dry. You can see this connection if you compare the world climate zones map on page 11 in this chapter with the world population density map on page 35 in Chapter 2.

How people live and work. The type of housing people live in, the clothes they wear, and the kind of work they do, all depend in part on the climate of their region. The physical structure of the land also can affect what work people do. For example, large-scale farming is an option in plains areas, but not in mountain regions.

Agriculture. To a large extent, climate dictates what crops can or can't be successfully grown in an area. Using technology, such as artificial irrigation or greenhouses, can change the impact of weather and climate to a degree. However, agriculture is most successful when crops are naturally suited to the area in which they are grown.

Transportation. An area's climate and topography can dictate which forms of transportation are used there. For example, dogsleds are an obvious choice in Arctic areas, while camels or elephants are well suited to travel in hot, arid conditions. More roads and railroads will be built in areas that have a level terrain, as opposed to mountainous areas.

Economy. Some areas, such as deserts, have little or no natural resources. These areas have a climate or topography that doesn't allow for extensive agriculture or a developed transportation system. Such harsh regions will probably be poorer than areas that can support industry, large-scale agriculture, or other means of making a living and engaging in trade.

The Land of Australia and the South Pacific and the People

Australians who live where the climate is harsh have found ways to adapt. Perhaps the most unusual example is found in South Australia. One of the world's largest opal mines is located there, in the town of Coober Pedy—the *underground* town of Coober Pedy. Houses and stores alike have been built below ground to insulate everyone from temperatures that commonly hit 120 degrees Fahrenheit (49 degrees Celsius).

Thatched houses offer cool living quarters on hot South Pacific islands. For added ventilation, the houses may be raised on stilts. This is also done on those islands where flooding from tropical storms is a common occurrence.

The Land of Australia and the South Pacific and the Economy

As the map on page 34 shows, Australia has six states and two federal territories. The states are New South Wales, Victoria, South Australia, Western Australia, Queensland, and Tasmania. The territories, which are self-governing but do not have states rights, are Northern Territory and Australian Capital Territory.

If you look at the climate map of Australia on page 16, you may conclude that most of the land is not especially useful or valuable because so much of the continent is arid or semi-arid. However, Australia's thriving economy is based mainly on the land; specifically, on raising livestock and on mining. Raising cattle is a major economic activity. And, as you can see by the land use map on page 24, cattle ranches are widely distributed around the continent. However, different types of cattle are raised in different climate regions. Brahmin cattle, native to India, are raised in the hot, humid areas of northern Australia. In the more temperate southeast, you'll find European cattle breeds.

In contrast to Australia, New Zealand's economy depends on agriculture almost exclusively because there are few mineral resources in the country, as you can see on the map on page 26.

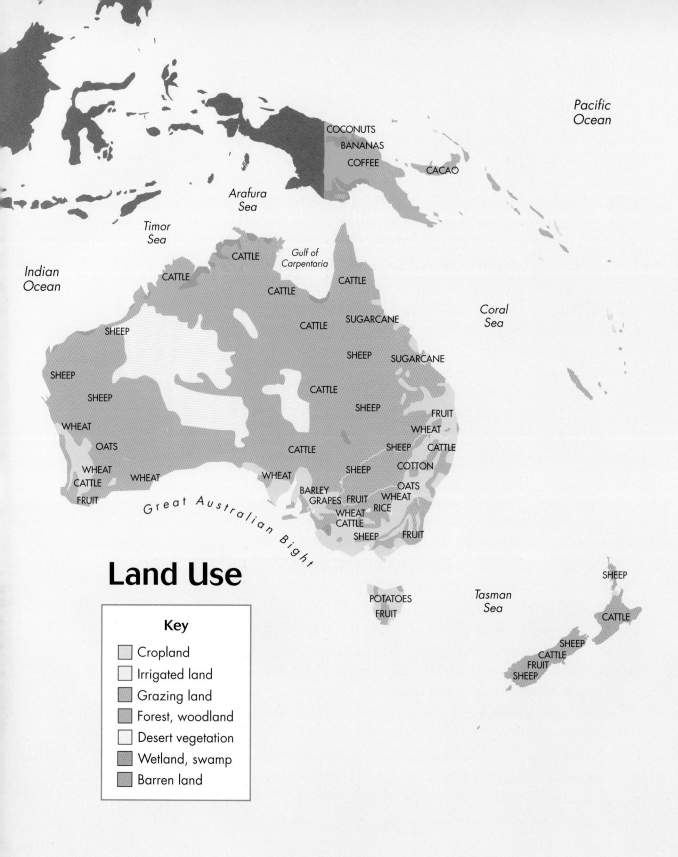

Land Use

Key

- Cropland
- Irrigated land
- Grazing land
- Forest, woodland
- Desert vegetation
- Wetland, swamp
- Barren land

Pacific Ocean

Arafura Sea

Timor Sea

Indian Ocean

Gulf of Carpentaria

Coral Sea

Great Australian Bight

Tasman Sea

COCONUTS
BANANAS
COFFEE
CACAO

CATTLE
CATTLE
CATTLE
CATTLE
CATTLE
SUGARCANE
SHEEP
SUGARCANE
SHEEP
CATTLE
SHEEP
SHEEP
SHEEP
SHEEP
FRUIT
WHEAT
WHEAT
OATS
WHEAT
CATTLE
FRUIT
CATTLE
SHEEP
CATTLE
WHEAT
COTTON
OATS
WHEAT
RICE
BARLEY
GRAPES
FRUIT
WHEAT
CATTLE
SHEEP
FRUIT

POTATOES
FRUIT

SHEEP
CATTLE
SHEEP
CATTLE
FRUIT
SHEEP

Crops

Australia's most important crops are sugarcane and wheat. Sugarcane plantations are found primarily on the humid northeast coast of the state of Queensland. There are large wheat farms in the southeast and the southwest. Australia ranks as a leading world exporter of wheat.

Queensland's tropical coastal climate is also perfect for growing fruits such as bananas and pineapples. Cotton, oats, and rice come from the southeast coastal farm belt. Peach, plum and citrus-fruit orchards are found in the southwest, and apples, pears, and potatoes are important products in Tasmania. Australian vineyards, particularly those in South Australia, near Adelaide, produce grapes for making wines that are sold worldwide.

Subsistence farming—growing crops for personal use—is common in most of the rest of the South Pacific. On some islands, such as Papua New Guinea, there are coffee, cocoa, coconut, or banana plantations where food is raised for export.

Livestock

Australia's pastures are used to graze sheep as well as cattle. With more than 100 million sheep, Australia ranks as the world's leading sheep-raising country and wool producer.

Sheep and cattle ranches are located primarily in the drier areas of the country, where they cover huge tracts of land. In the state of Western Australia, some sheep ranches are as large as the state of Kentucky, in the United States. The ranches need to be this big because in the driest grazing areas, it takes a lot of land to feed a single animal.

◄◄ **Opposite:** *Most of Australia's land is used for raising sheep and cattle.*

▼ **Below:** *Cattle graze at a ranch—which Australians call a "station"—in South Australia.*

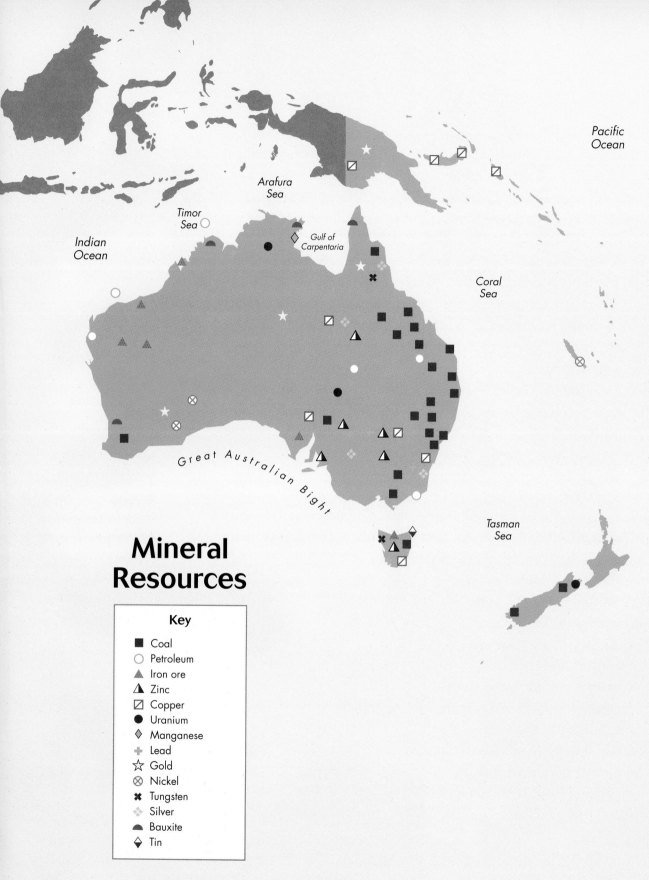

Mineral Resources

Key

- ■ Coal
- ○ Petroleum
- ▲ Iron ore
- △ Zinc
- ▨ Copper
- ● Uranium
- ◆ Manganese
- ✚ Lead
- ☆ Gold
- ⊗ Nickel
- ✖ Tungsten
- ✦ Silver
- ◗ Bauxite
- ◈ Tin

Pacific Ocean

Arafura Sea

Timor Sea

Indian Ocean

Gulf of Carpentaria

Coral Sea

Great Australian Bight

Tasman Sea

26

New Zealand is also a major sheep- and cattle-raising country. In fact, there are about 25 times more cattle and sheep than there are people! Unlike Australia, where sheep are raised primarily for their wool, in New Zealand they are raised mostly for meat. The country ranks as a leading world exporter of lamb and mutton.

Forestry

Timber is important to the economy of several islands, including New Zealand, Papua New Guinea, and the Solomon Islands.

Mineral Resources

Australia contains a wide variety of minerals, and as you can see by the map on the opposite page, the deposits are extensive. Ever since gold was discovered in the mid-1800s, mining has been an important economic activity. Today, Australia is among the world's major mining countries.

Although mineral deposits are found throughout the continent, Western Australia, Queensland, and New South Wales have the heaviest concentrations.

Australia ranks first in the production of bauxite, which is used to make aluminum. It is mined chiefly in Queensland, Western Australia, and the Northern Territory. Australia is also a top producer of lead and zinc, which are mined extensively in New South Wales. Zinc is used as a protective coating for iron and steel.

Coal is mined extensively in both New South Wales and Queensland. The majority of the iron ore, nickel, and gold comes from Western Australia. Manganese is mined only in the Northern Territory, and tin is produced primarily in Tasmania. Australia is a leading producer of most of the other minerals shown on the map. The exception is uranium. Some uranium is mined in Australia, but overall, the country contains the world's largest undeveloped deposits.

New Zealand has few important minerals, and valuable mineral deposits are scarce among the other islands of the South Pacific. Major exceptions include New Caledonia, which is one of the world's

◀◀ *Opposite: Papua New Guinea has significant deposits of gold and copper.*

leading nickel-mining countries, and Papua New Guinea, with its copper and gold mines.

Within the territorial ocean waters of Papua New Guinea are still more deposits of gold and copper as well as silver. An Australian mining company has claimed 2,000 square miles (5,180 square kilometers) of mineral deposits in the deep sea—the first claim to minerals in the deep sea that has ever been made. Miners say that the mineral deposits, discovered in 1991 and 1993, are worth billions of dollars. They are in rocky volcanic outcroppings about 1 mile (1.6 kilometers) below the surface of the water. The company that has claimed these deposits is waiting for approval from authorities before they begin to mine the minerals—a process that will be very expensive.

Energy Production and Consumption

Looking at the energy production map on page 30, you can see that Australia's principal energy resources are coal and natural gas. Important gas fields are located off the northwest coast, in South Australia, eastern Queensland, and off the coast of Victoria. Almost half of Australia's petroleum comes from Victoria's offshore oil basin. Major coal fields are found in the eastern and the far southwestern portions of the country.

New Zealand, too, depends on coal and natural gas for energy. However, the country's fast-moving rivers and streams provide much energy in the form of hydroelectric power, which is also the case in Tasmania. Many of the other islands in the South Pacific do not have the resources to produce their own energy. Instead, they must import fuel.

Look at the energy consumption map on page 31. Transportation, mining, and air-conditioning account in large part for Australia's heavy energy consumption. New Zealand's overall energy consumption is less than Australia's for several reasons.

While New Zealand uses a lot of energy for transportation, this is offset by the country's more temperate climate (which means less

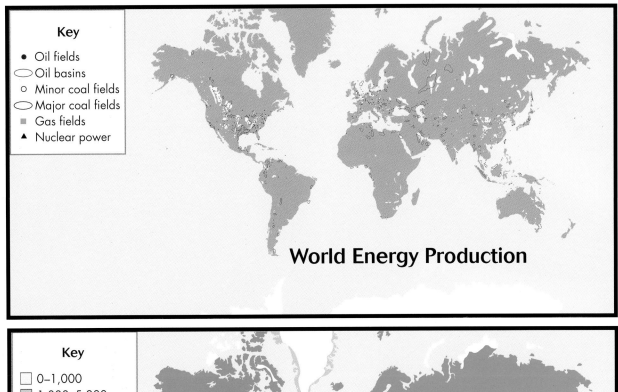

Key

- • Oil fields
- ◯ Oil basins
- ◦ Minor coal fields
- ◯ Major coal fields
- ▪ Gas fields
- ▲ Nuclear power

World Energy Production

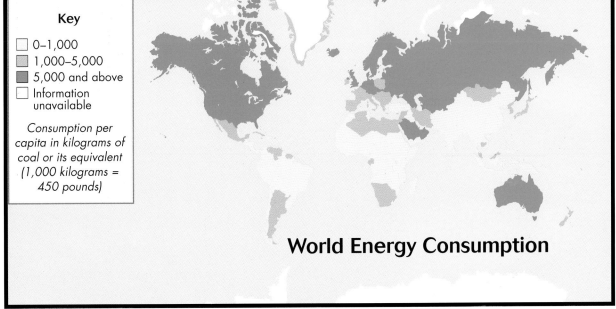

Key

- ☐ 0–1,000
- ▨ 1,000–5,000
- ■ 5,000 and above
- ☐ Information unavailable

Consumption per capita in kilograms of coal or its equivalent (1,000 kilograms = 450 pounds)

World Energy Consumption

air-conditioning) and its modest need for energy to support mining and manufacturing. Papua New Guinea, New Caledonia, and Fiji, as well as the rest of the South Pacific, consume the least amount of energy because of their smaller populations and less overall need. To see how Australia and the rest of the South Pacific compare to the rest of the world in energy production and consumption, see the maps above.

▲ *Above: Australia produces and consumes more energy per capita than any other country south of the equator.*

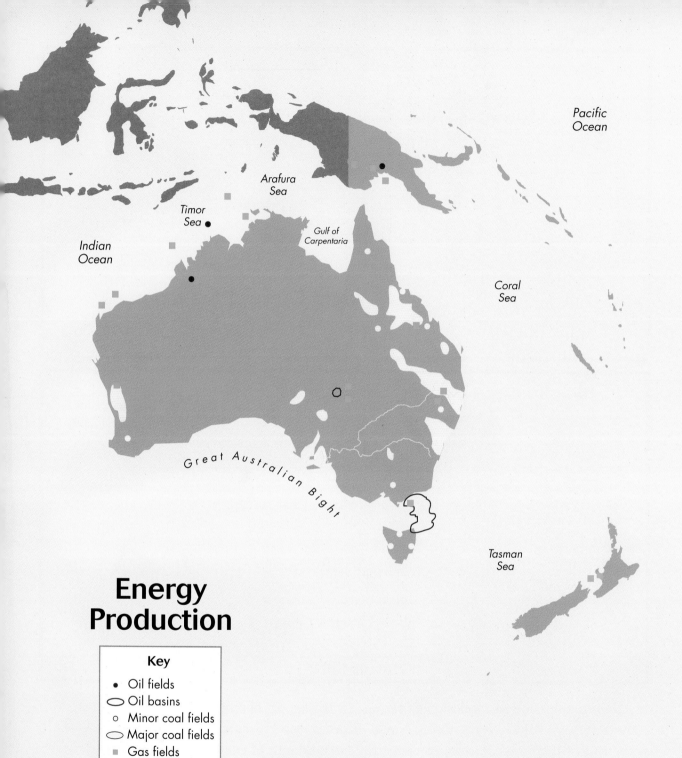

Pacific
Ocean

Arafura
Sea

Timor
Sea

Indian
Ocean

Gulf of
Carpentaria

Coral
Sea

Great Australian Bight

Tasman
Sea

Energy
Production

Key
• Oil fields
⬭ Oil basins
○ Minor coal fields
⬯ Major coal fields
▪ Gas fields

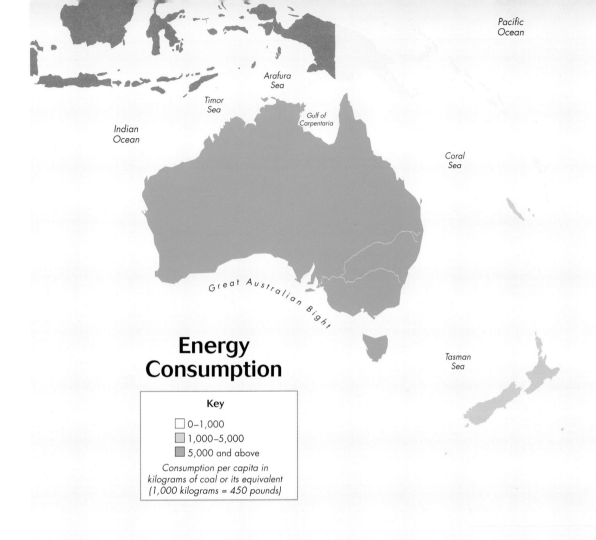

Energy Consumption

Key

☐ 0–1,000
▨ 1,000–5,000
■ 5,000 and above

Consumption per capita in kilograms of coal or its equivalent (1,000 kilograms = 450 pounds)

Pacific Ocean

Arafura Sea

Timor Sea

Indian Ocean

Gulf of Carpentaria

Coral Sea

Great Australian Bight

Tasman Sea

Finally, take a look at the map of fossil fuel emissions on page 33. Here you can see how Australia and the South Pacific are affected by the burning of coal and oil and compare them to other areas of the world. Harmful emissions from the burning of fossil fuels contribute to environmental problems such as global warming, the destruction of the ozone layer, and acid rain.

The Environment

Australia's environmental problems are shown on the environmental damage map on page 32. As you can see, the three most pressing problems are coastal pollution, human-induced salinization, and human-induced desertification.

▲ *Above:* Papua New Guinea and the smaller islands to the southeast are light energy consumers.

◀◀ *Opposite:* The large oil basin north of Tasmania provides Australia with half of the petroleum that it uses.

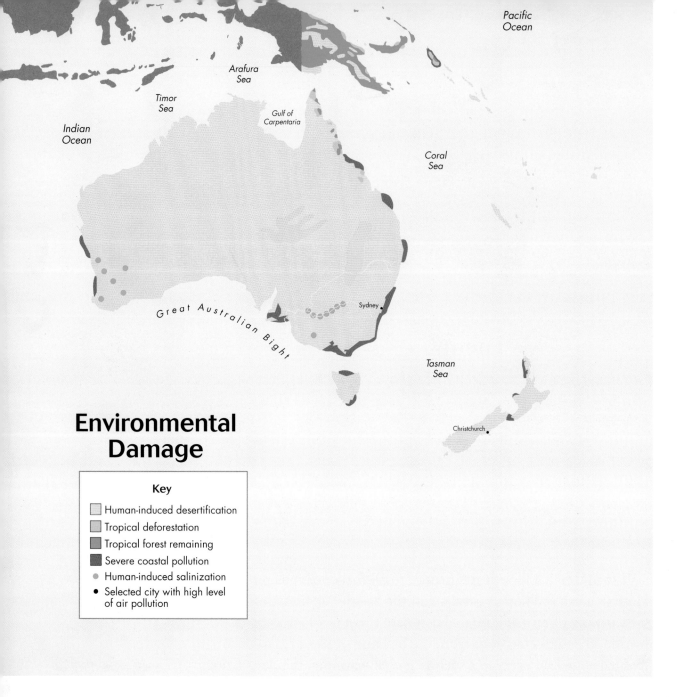

Pacific
Ocean

Arafura
Sea

Timor
Sea

Gulf of
Carpentaria

Indian
Ocean

Coral
Sea

Great Australian Bight

Sydney

Tasman
Sea

Christchurch

Environmental Damage

Key

- Human-induced desertification
- Tropical deforestation
- Tropical forest remaining
- Severe coastal pollution
- Human-induced salinization
- Selected city with high level of air pollution

▲ *Above:* Australia suffers from coastal pollution near its largest cities.

Compare this map with the population density map on page 47. Almost every polluted area corresponds to an area of particularly dense population. These cities are also visited by many tourists each year. High concentrations of people pollute the land and water with garbage and sewage. In addition, Australia's population centers are also the country's manufacturing centers. A triple threat!

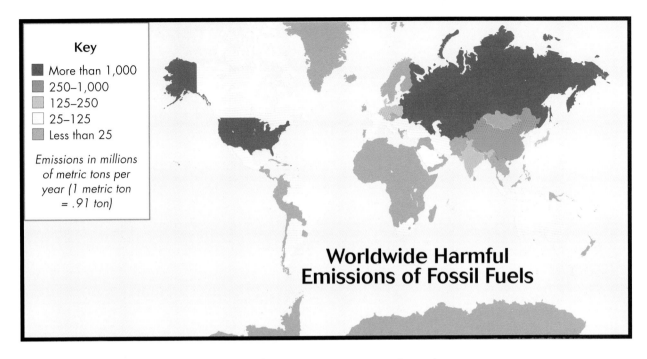

Key

- More than 1,000
- 250–1,000
- 125–250
- 25–125
- Less than 25

Emissions in millions of metric tons per year (1 metric ton = .91 ton)

Worldwide Harmful Emissions of Fossil Fuels

The points of human-induced salinization are areas where intensive irrigation has washed the nutrients from the soil, leaving it encrusted with salts. Salinized land is unsuitable for crops or livestock.

Desertification can result from either overgrazing or intensive farming methods used because of the pressure to increase agricultural production. Both of these causes are at work in Australia.

▲ **Above:** *Australia emits a relatively small amount of fossil fuels.*

A Closer Look

You can learn a lot about what a place is like by looking at different kinds of maps, one at a time. However, by comparing the information presented in two or more maps, you can discover something about how and why it got that way.

Compare the climate and land use maps in this chapter. How does the climate map help explain the way the land is used? Now compare the climate map and the population density map in Chapter 2 on page 47. What conclusions can you draw about where people choose to live?

Pacific
Ocean

**Papua
New
Guinea**

**Solomon
Islands**

*Arafura
Sea*

*Coral
Sea*

*Timor
Sea*

*Gulf of
Carpentaria*

Vanuatu

Fiji

*Indian
Ocean*

Northern
Territory

**New
Caledonia**

AUSTRALIA

Queensland

Western Australia

South
Australia

New South Wales

Australian
Capital Territory

Area of Detail

*Tasman
Sea*

Victoria

*North
Island*

Great Australian Bight

Political Map

Tasmania

*South
Island*

**New
Zealand**

Scale

1,000 km

1,000 mi.

*Stewart
Island*

New South Wales

**Australian
Capital Territory**

Victoria

Chapter 2

Mapping People, Cultures, and the Political World

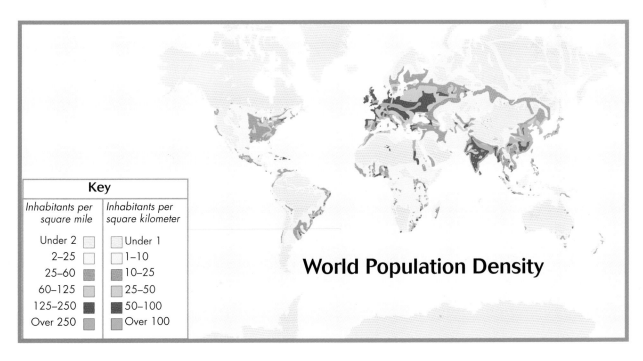

Key

Inhabitants per square mile	Inhabitants per square kilometer
Under 2	Under 1
2–25	1–10
25–60	10–25
60–125	25–50
125–250	50–100
Over 250	Over 100

World Population Density

Maps can reveal much more about a place than simply what it is like physically. They can also tell you a great deal about the political divisions of the area. Maps can inform you about the cultures and customs of the people who live there, as well. They can show the languages spoken in a region, the religions people identify with, and the places where most people live.

◀◀ *Opposite: By 1911, the political map of Australia looked just as it does today.*

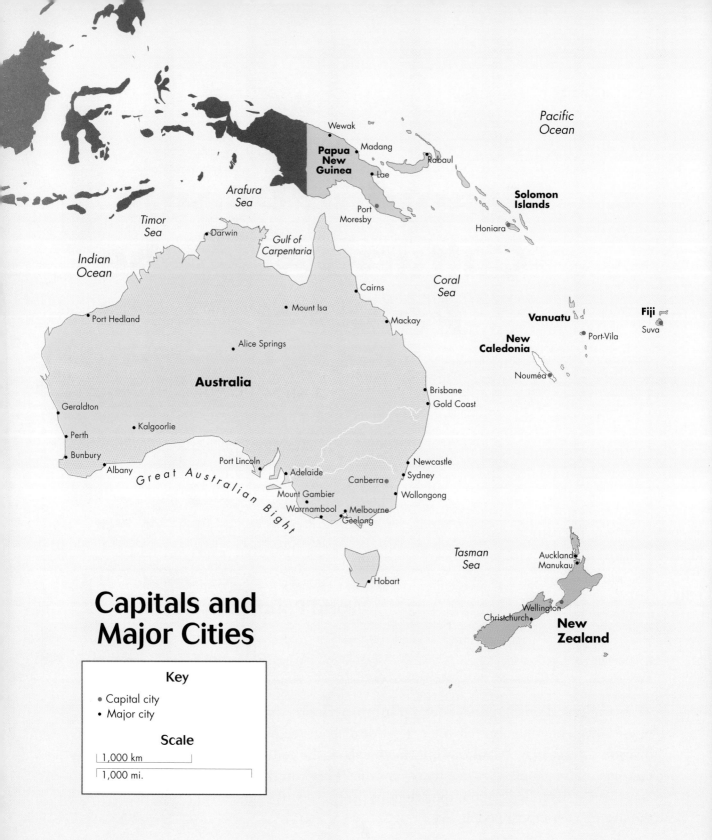

Pacific
Ocean

Wewak
Madang
Papua New Guinea
Rabaul
Lae

Solomon Islands

Arafura Sea

Port Moresby

Honiara

Timor Sea

Darwin

Gulf of Carpentaria

Indian Ocean

Coral Sea

Cairns

Mount Isa

Mackay

Vanuatu

Fiji

Port Hedland

Alice Springs

Port-Vila

Suva

Australia

New Caledonia

Geraldton

Nouméa

Perth
Kalgoorlie

Bunbury
Albany

Great Australian Bight

Port Lincoln

Adelaide

Mount Gambier
Warrnambool
Melbourne
Geelong

Brisbane
Gold Coast

Newcastle
Sydney
Canberra
Wollongong

Tasman Sea

Auckland
Manukau

Hobart

Wellington

Christchurch

New Zealand

Capitals and Major Cities

Key

• Capital city

• Major city

Scale

1,000 km

1,000 mi.

The Political World: Dividing the Land

Political maps such as the one on page 34 are familiar to everyone. In these, there is no attempt to show what an area physically looks like. Rather, a political map shows the boundaries that separate countries (or states and provinces). Colors are used to distinguish one country from another. A political map may also show capitals and major cities, as the map on the opposite page does.

Boundaries are artificial; that is, they are created, set, and changed by people. Conquests, wars, and treaties have all caused boundary changes. Political maps can, therefore, also be a guide to the history of a region.

Geographers keep track of boundary changes, and country and city name changes, as they occur, so that new, up-to-date political maps can be created as soon as possible.

The Political World: Nature's Influence

The political world is not entirely separate from the natural world. Rivers or mountains may dictate where boundaries are set. Also, if there is a wealth of natural resources in one location, people may try to set boundaries that put all or most of those resources within their own country's borders. Cities, too, are often located according to natural features. Comparing climate and major city maps will show that cities tend to cluster along coastlines or major waterways, and in areas that have less severe climates.

The History of Australia and the South Pacific

The Original Inhabitants

Many islands of the South Pacific were inhabited thousands of years before Europeans discovered them. For example, New Guinea is thought to have been occupied 50,000 years ago, and Australia's Aborigines came from Southeast Asia to that continent about 40,000 years ago. On the other hand, the first settlers didn't arrive in New

◄◄ *Opposite: The capital city of Canberra is one of Australia's few inland cities.*

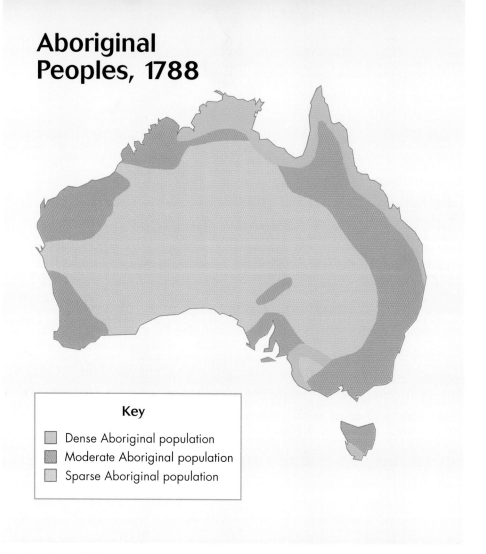

Aboriginal Peoples, 1788

Key

- Dense Aboriginal population
- Moderate Aboriginal population
- Sparse Aboriginal population

▶ *Right: During the late eighteenth century, Australia's Aboriginal population was densest on the north coast.*

Zealand until about A.D. 100, and the Maori—today's native New Zealanders—arrived about A.D. 800.

It is believed that people came to the Pacific islands from Southeast Asia. In general, the closer, western islands were settled first; later, the inhabitants of these islands migrated toward the east.

European explorers and settlers changed the lives of native islanders not only by introducing new beliefs and value systems to their culture, but also by taking over their land. In Australia, for example, there were about 750,000 Aborigines when Europeans established their first settlement in 1788. And, as you can see by the map above, the Aborigines lived throughout the continent. Today there are about 270,000 Aborigines living in Australia, with large concentrations found in Northern Territory and South Australia.

European Exploration

European exploration of the South Pacific began in 1520, when Ferdinand Magellan sailed west across the Pacific Ocean from the tip of South America. Other navigators soon crisscrossed the ocean on their way to the East Indies from South America. During the 1500s, various islands were discovered by the Europeans, but their positions in the ocean were not well mapped because mapmakers and explorers lacked precise tools for establishing longitude.

The maps did show something unusual, though. In the second century, Greek geographer Ptolemy thought that a huge landmass had to cover the bottom of Earth in order to balance the northern part of the world. Otherwise, he said, the world would be top-heavy and tip over. This landmass was called *Terra Australis Incognita*, which is Latin for "Unknown Southern Land." Maps of the 1500s and 1600s showed this landmass below South America and Africa, although no one had ever seen it.

During the early 1600s, Dutch sailors sighted, explored, and mapped sections of Australia's north and west coasts. They called the area New Holland and thought it was part of Ptolemy's great Southern Land, Terra Australis.

In 1642, the Dutch navigator Abel Tasman discovered land that he thought was another part of the Terra Australis. It was actually the island that was later named Tasmania in his honor. Sailing east, Tasman discovered New Zealand, where Maoris attacked his landing party and killed some of the men. In 1644, Tasman made a voyage to New Guinea. On that same trip he sailed along and mapped much of New Holland's (Australia's) northwest coast.

From what they had seen of New Holland, the Dutch were not much impressed with this new land—a mix of barren desert and swampy rain forest. Because of New Holland's unwelcoming topography and the hostile natives of New Zealand, it was to be more than 125 years before the next major European exploration of the region.

Ptolemy

Captain James Cook

In 1768, the English explorer and mapmaker Captain James Cook was sent by the British Navy to the South Pacific. One of his missions was to look for Terra Australis. (The English were not sure the Dutch had actually found it.) Cook found no sign of that land but, in 1769, he arrived in New Zealand and claimed it for Great Britain. Cook and his crew made friends with the Maori, and spent several months charting New Zealand's North and South Islands.

From there he sailed west and, in 1770, became the first European to explore Australia's east coast. He mapped the coastline and claimed this fertile area for Great Britain, naming it New South Wales.

Cook made a second voyage to the South Pacific that lasted from 1772 to 1775. For the first time, Cook had a chronometer—an instrument that enabled him to determine the longitude of his positions. On this voyage, he visited and precisely mapped the locations of many South Pacific islands, including New Caledonia. His work changed the map face of the South Pacific—and the world—for all time.

Australia Becomes a Colony

In 1788, eleven British ships arrived on Australia's east coast carrying sailors, soldiers, government officials—and convicts. It had been decided that New South Wales would be used as a prison colony. The group settled and built what would eventually become the city of Sydney. Later, prison settlements were also established near what is now Brisbane, in Western Australia, and on Tasmania.

In the 1790s, free settlers also began arriving in Australia. Even then, however, no one had yet sailed all the way around the continent. Most of the south coast and part of the north coast were still unmapped. The country's true size and shape were unknown, although the land appeared on various world maps. It was not until 1803 that explorers finally circumnavigated (sailed around) Australia, and the charting of its coastline was completed.

Whalers, Traders, and Missionaries in New Zealand

During the late 1700s, the waters around New Zealand attracted whale and seal hunters from many countries, and whaling stations were set up on the country's North and South Islands. Traders visited New Zealand to barter with the Maori for flax (used to make rope) and timber; they travelled to other Pacific islands for products such as coconut oil.

In the early 1800s, European missionaries came to the islands to spread Christianity. Settlers arrived, too. They came to New Zealand to escape poor living conditions back home (particularly England), and to other islands to establish plantations. In 1840, Britain signed the Treaty of Waitangi with the Maori, and New Zealand became a British colony. By the late 1800s, most South Pacific islands were under the control of Great Britain, France, or Germany.

Into the Outback

Although Australia's whole coastline was charted by 1803, more than a century passed before the continent was completely explored. As you can see by the maps on page 42, the southeast part of Australia was explored first. Later, exploration opened up the south and the southwestern coastal regions, followed by the east and north coasts, and a good portion of the interior.

Soldiers, scientists, trained surveyors, and adventurers all had a hand in exploring Australia's interior (which is also called the "outback") and committing it to maps. There were some surprises. For example, people thought that there had to be an inland lake or sea to account for the west-flowing rivers. However, expeditions in the first half of the 1800s proved that no such body of water existed.

Explorers of the outback suffered many hardships because of the heat and lack of water. In 1860, an expedition led by Robert Burke and John Wills set out to cross Australia from south to north. Although Burke and Wills made it to the Gulf of Carpentaria, their camels died on the way, and they themselves died of starvation on the return trip.

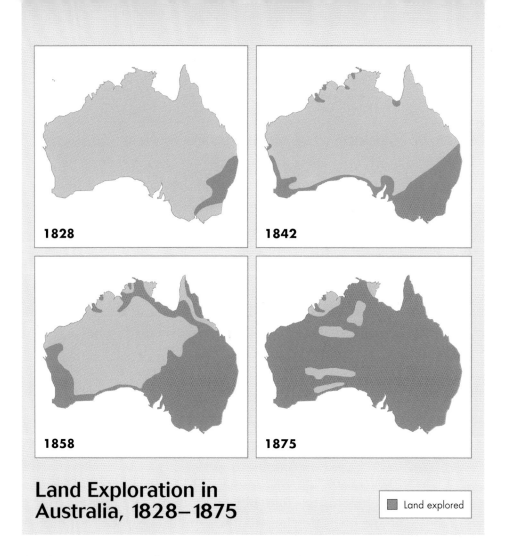

1828

1842

1858

1875

Land Exploration in Australia, 1828–1875

Land explored

▶ *Right: As late as 1875, portions of Australia's outback were unexplored.*

Independence for Australia and New Zealand

Throughout the 1800s, Australia existed as separate colonies of free British settlers. Then, a constitutional convention was convened in 1897 and 1898. The resulting constitution was approved by the people of Australia and Great Britain, and on January 1, 1901, Australia gained its independence. It became a member of the British Commonwealth of Nations, which share political and economic interests.

Australia included the six states in existence today. In 1911, the Northern Territory and the Australian Capital Territory were established, and the political map of Australia looked as it does now (see page 34). In 1907, New Zealand became an independent country within the British Commonwealth as well.

The Colonization of Other South Pacific Islands

Throughout the late 1700s and into the 1800s, European explorers, traders, and missionaries visited the islands of the South Pacific. Eventually, most islands were claimed by one country or another—and sometimes more than one at a time. For example, in 1884, the northern half of Papua New Guinea was claimed by Germany and the southern half by Great Britain. In 1906, Great Britain gave control of its portion to Australia and, in 1918, Australia gained the German portion by a League of Nations mandate. Papua New Guinea became an independent nation in 1975. In contrast, New Caledonia has been a French territory since it came under that country's control in 1853. Although French territorial status is agreeable to the French people who live in New Caledonia, the Kanaks (native Melanesians) would like the country to be independent.

Population, Language, and Religion

Political maps tell us about the boundaries of a nation, but not about the lives of its inhabitants. Maps that focus on population, language, and religion tell us more about a country's people. Most countries' governments conduct a census (population count) on some sort of

▼ *Below: The populations of Australia and New Zealand are growing more slowly than those of other countries south of the equator.*

Key

Decrease
0–1%
1–2%
2–3%
>3%

(Does not include effects of migration)

World Annual Average Population Growth

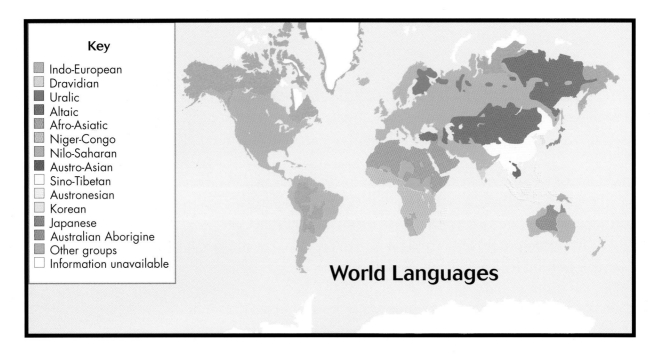

Key

- Indo-European
- Dravidian
- Uralic
- Altaic
- Afro-Asiatic
- Niger-Congo
- Nilo-Saharan
- Austro-Asian
- Sino-Tibetan
- Austronesian
- Korean
- Japanese
- Australian Aborigine
- Other groups
- Information unavailable

World Languages

▲ *Above:* Indo-European languages are dominant on parts of every continent but Africa.

▼ *Below:* The South Pacific represents fewer religions than nearby Asia.

regular basis. The United States, for example, has conducted a census every ten years since 1790.

Census figures are used to make maps that show how population is distributed. The world population density map on page 35 is one such map. By compiling statistics over a period of years—from census and birth to death records—geographers can make predictions regarding population growth, as shown on the map on page 43.

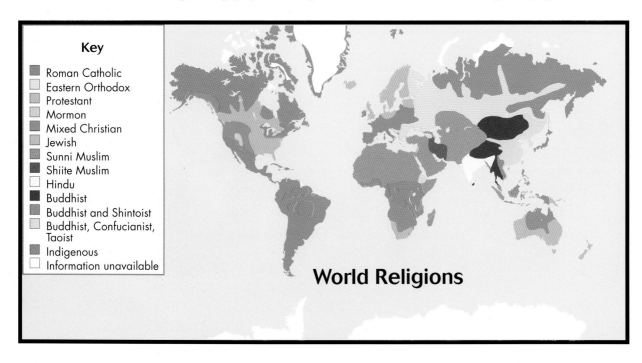

Key

- Roman Catholic
- Eastern Orthodox
- Protestant
- Mormon
- Mixed Christian
- Jewish
- Sunni Muslim
- Shiite Muslim
- Hindu
- Buddhist
- Buddhist and Shintoist
- Buddhist, Confucianist, Taoist
- Indigenous
- Information unavailable

World Religions

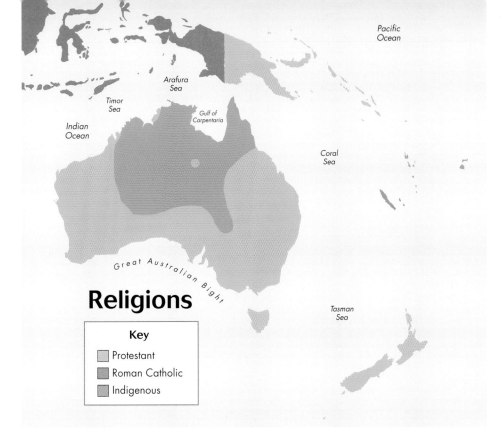

Religions

Key
- Protestant
- Roman Catholic
- Indigenous

Pacific Ocean

Arafura Sea

Timor Sea

Indian Ocean

Gulf of Carpentaria

Coral Sea

Great Australian Bight

Tasman Sea

◀ **Left:** *The predominance of Catholicism in New Caledonia reflects the influence of the country's early French settlers.*

Because many different languages may be spoken in any one country, it is difficult to map language distribution precisely. However, large areas that represent language families can be mapped, as shown on the map on the opposite page. In the same way, predominant religions of an area can also be mapped, as shown on the world religions map on the same page.

The Religions of Australia and the South Pacific

Look at the map above. You will see that Protestant religions are in the majority in Australia, New Zealand, and Papua New Guinea. New Caledonia, on the other hand, is primarily Roman Catholic. This distribution reflects the particular European settlement of each island.

The early colonists of Australia and New Zealand were from England, which is primarily a Protestant country. Papua New Guinea was originally colonized by German and British settlers. New Caledonia, however, was colonized by France, where Catholicism is the primary religion.

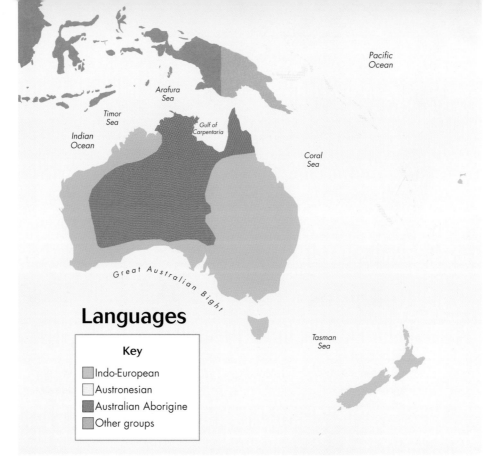

Languages

Key
- Indo-European
- Austronesian
- Australian Aborigine
- Other groups

▶**Right:** *Most people who live on the smaller islands of the South Pacific speak Austronesian languages.*

This same pattern is seen throughout the Pacific, particularly in the larger island groups where European colonists established large, permanent settlements. Traditional native religious beliefs may be observed by small groups of people, especially those living outside the cities. On islands without a large European population, indigenous religions may be practiced exclusively. Look again at the religions map. The area of Australia where indigenous religions dominate, colored pink, is where most non-urban Aboriginals live.

The Languages of Australia and the South Pacific

The majority of Australians and New Zealanders speak English. English is an Indo-European language, which is indicated in green on the languages map. Mirroring the religions map, the languages map above shows that Australian Aborigine dialects are spoken in the out-back area, where the country's rural, indigenous peoples live.

Because New Caledonia is a territory of France, and French is also an Indo-European language, you might expect New Caledonia to

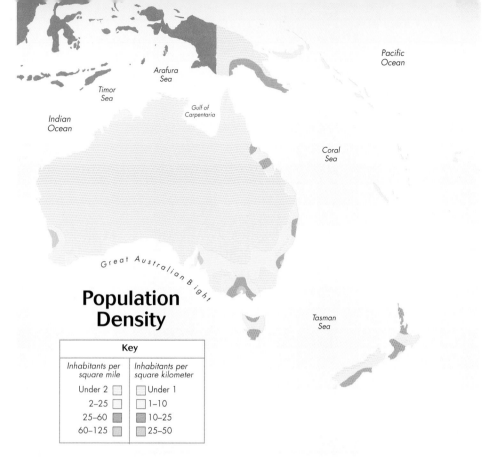

Population Density

Key	
Inhabitants per square mile	Inhabitants per square kilometer
Under 2 ☐	☐ Under 1
2–25 ☐	☐ 1–10
25–60 ■	■ 10–25
60–125 ☐	■ 25–50

◀ *Left: Papua New Guinea's south coast is far more densely populated than its north coast.*

be colored green, too. Although French is the official language of the territory, French-speaking people do not make up the majority of the population. Most New Caledonians speak a Melanesian or Polynesian dialect, which are part of the Austronesian language family. Most other Pacific island languages also fall under this heading.

In Papua New Guinea, native people belong to thousands of different groups and speak more than 600 different languages. Europeans are in the minority. Although English is an official language, most residents of Papua New Guinea speak a second official language called Pidgin—a unique mixture of simplified English and Melanesian dialects.

Population Growth and Density

With the exception of Antarctica, Australia has the smallest population of any continent in the world. In 1997, the population was 18.5 million people. Australia is the most populous country in the South Pacific, however. Papua New Guinea, the second-most populous

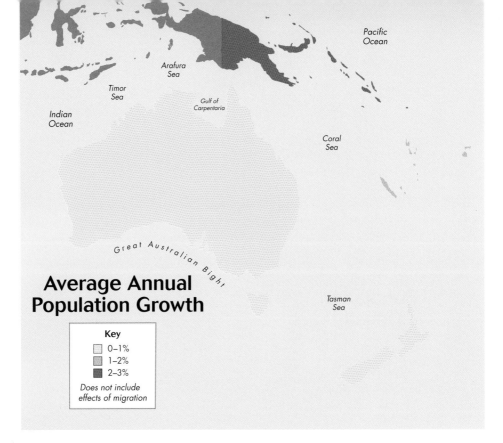

Average Annual Population Growth

Key
- ☐ 0–1%
- ▦ 1–2%
- ■ 2–3%

Does not include effects of migration

country in the South Pacific, has about 4.5 million people, and New Zealand, a little more than 3.5 million.

As you can see from the population density map on page 47, Australia's population is very unevenly distributed. Most people live close to the coast, in the northeast, southeast, and southwest on the mainland, and on the island of Tasmania. The heaviest population concentration is on the mainland in the southeast, around the cities of Brisbane, Sydney, Melbourne, and Adelaide.

New Zealand's population is densest on North Island. On South Island, which is very mountainous, the population is concentrated where there are plains and rolling hills.

The populations of both Australia and New Zealand are highly urban. More than 80 percent of Australians and more than 75 percent of New Zealanders live in or near a city.

Among the South Pacific islands, New Calendonia's population is fairly evenly distributed. The population of Papua New Guinea is most heavily concentrated along the south coast, however, where the country's capital and most developed areas lie.

Population growth is relatively low in the South Pacific, as you can see on the map on page 48. The populations of Australia and New Zealand are increasing by only 1 percent a year or less. An exception to this low population growth is Papua New Guinea, where the population is growing by between 2 and 3 percent a year. Use the world map on page 43 to see how this compares with other areas of the world.

Per Capita GDP

Gross Domestic Product (GDP) is the total output of a country—all products and labor. Dividing the value of a country's GDP by its population gives the per capita (per person) GDP. This figure represents the average annual income of that country's people. Generally speaking, more industrialized countries have a higher GDP—and a better economy—than less industrialized countries.

Australia and New Zealand are not highly industrialized countries. They are nevertheless considered developed countries, and they have high standards of living. Australia's estimated 1995 per capita GDP was $21,100, and New Zealand's was $18,100. A few islands of the South Pacific have mineral resources that are mined and exported, contributing to a moderately healthy GDP. For example, New Caledonia's estimated 1995 per capita GDP of $8,000 is directly related to its nickel deposits. However, most islands of the South Pacific do not have developed economies that translate into significant annual incomes.

A Closer Look

Climate is one of the things that has a bearing on how people live. Compare the Aboriginal peoples map on page 38 with the climate map on page 16. Can you see why the Aborigines were originally hunter-gatherers, and not farmers like the Europeans who came later and settled the southeastern and eastern areas of Australia?

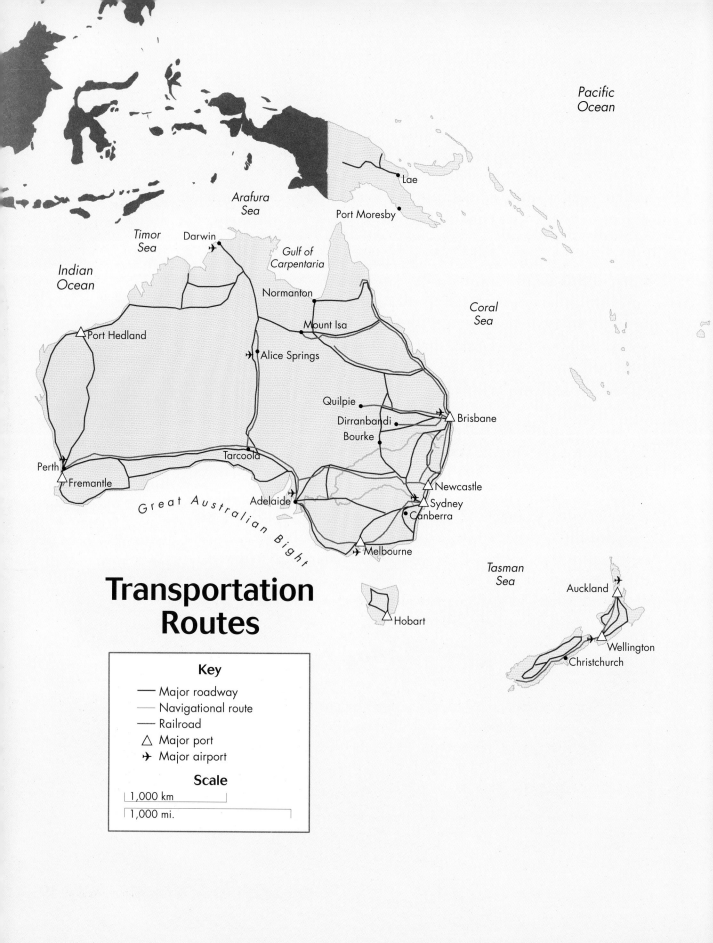

Pacific
Ocean

Lae

Port Moresby

*Arafura
Sea*

*Timor
Sea*

Darwin

*Gulf of
Carpentaria*

Normanton

*Indian
Ocean*

Mount Isa

*Coral
Sea*

Port Hedland

Alice Springs

Quilpie

Dirranbandi

Brisbane

Bourke

Perth

Tarcoola

Fremantle

Adelaide

Newcastle

Sydney

Canberra

Great Australian Bight

Melbourne

*Tasman
Sea*

Auckland

Transportation
Routes

Hobart

Wellington

Christchurch

Key

— Major roadway
— Navigational route
— Railroad
△ Major port
✈ Major airport

Scale

| 1,000 km
| 1,000 mi.

3

Mapping the World Through Which We Move

In addition to showing us the physical and political characteristics of the world, maps can also have a more practical, "hands on" purpose: they can assist us in moving through our world. Whether that world is an entire continent, a single city, or the second floor of an art museum, different maps provide us with the information we need to get from one point to another.

Maps Show the Way

Whenever we want to get from one place to another, maps can help us plan our routes by showing the options that are available. Maps show where roads are located and what kind of roads they are. They can also tell us whether we can take an airplane, train, bus, or other form of transportation to get there. Once we reach our destination, maps again can help us plan how best to get around—on foot, by car, or by some kind of public transportation.

Creating Road and City Maps

To create road maps and city maps, mapmakers (cartographers) look first for base data maps that accurately position points to be included

◄◄ *Opposite:* Australia *has only two significant navigational routes because most of its rivers are dry at least part of the year.*

on the new map. These base maps might be acquired from the federal government, states, or cities. Aerial photographs may be taken to show if, and how, any areas may have changed since the base map was made.

Then, cartographers contact agencies that can provide specific information about street names—the names that will be the most help to a person traveling in the area. Other agencies are contacted to determine which buildings or other points of interest are important and should be included on the map of the area. Field work—actually visiting the area being mapped—adds useful first-hand information.

The Importance of Scale

Choosing the right scale for a map is an important step in making sure that the map will be as useful as possible.

To help people find their way around downtown Boston, for example, a cartographer would design a large-scale map that gives a close-up view of all the streets. But suppose someone wanted to drive from Philadelphia in eastern Pennsylvania to Pittsburgh in western Pennsylvania. Then a small-scale road map of the entire state would be more helpful than large-scale maps of all the cities between Philadelphia and Pittsburgh.

Scale also plays an important part in determining what is shown on a map. The smaller the scale, the more carefully cartographers must pick and choose the details that are being included. Careful selection is needed in order to keep a map from becoming too cluttered.

The transportation and city maps in this chapter provide still more ways to look at and learn about the continent of Australia, other South Pacific countries, and various cities.

Transportation in Australia and the South Pacific

As you can see by the map on page 50, transportation routes in Australia are concentrated near the coast and in the southeast. In New Zealand, too, the primary routes tend to be coastal. This reflects the location of major cities and the lay of the land.

Roads

In Australia, roads provide the main overland transportation routes. Some of today's primary roadways roughly follow historic stock routes. During the 1800s, sheep and cattle were herded along these routes on their way to market in the capital cities. Major roadways link all of the mainland state capitals and largest cities. These roads are paved, but the smaller roads of the outback are not.

New Zealand's highway system is well developed: Both large and small towns are connected by paved roads. On Papua New Guinea, the main roads are in the capital and along the coast. The roads on other South Pacific islands are of varying quality and number. On some islands, there is only one main road—sometimes paved and sometimes not.

The majority of Australians and New Zealanders own cars. There is one car for every two people in Australia and one car for every three people in New Zealand. Trucks carry much of the freight in both countries. In Australia, "road trains" are a common means of moving cargo over long distances. A road train consists of a truck cab and several large trailers linked together. These units can be large enough to transport thousands of sheep from one point to another.

Railroads

In both Australia and New Zealand, railroads are used primarily for carrying freight. They are a means of moving mining and agricultural products from their sources to the country's port cities.

▼ *Below:* This monorail is part of Sydney's public transportation system.

Trains connect the major cities in both countries; in Australia, most rail lines run within 200 miles of the coast. The Indian-Pacific Railroad has the world's longest stretch of straight track—300 miles between Adelaide and Perth, across the Nullarbor Plain. There are commuter rail lines in Sydney and Melbourne, Australia's two largest cities.

Waterways

Most of Australia's rivers (identified as "navigational routes" on the map) are dry at least part of the year. For this reason, Australian rivers have not been as important for transportation as rivers in many other countries. The two main rivers, the Murray and the Darling, were used for transporting goods in the early and mid-1800s. However, once railroads were in place, they quickly replaced rivers as a favored means of transportation.

Oceans have always played a major part in Australia's transportation system, however. Before airplanes and automobiles became commonplace, ships routinely carried both passengers and cargo around Australia as well as overseas. Now ships are used primarily for transporting freight, not people. Among the most important port cities are Sydney, Newcastle, Melbourne, and Port Hedland.

Unlike Australia's rivers, New Zealand's rivers flow all year. However, they are not especially useful for transportation because their currents are fast and rough. Ocean shipping is used to transport cargo overseas and, as the map on page 50 shows, Auckland and Wellington are New Zealand's major seaports.

Travel between North and South Islands is done by ferry. These boats are extremely important links in the transportation system of New Zealand. They carry not only people and automobiles, but even railroad cars from one island to the other.

Pleasure boating is extremely popular among both Australians and New Zealanders. Throughout the rest of the South Pacific, the ocean is the only significant waterway, and ocean-going boats are an important means of basic transportation for people as well as cargo.

Airlines

Domestic air transportation is important in Australia both because of the size of the continent and the lack of other transportation in the outback. Special flying doctor services bring medical and dental help to people living in remote areas of Australia. For international travel, airlines regularly fly between Australia's major cities and airports around the world.

In New Zealand, Papua New Guinea, and on other South Pacific islands large enough to have an airport, airplanes are used mostly for international travel. Domestic flights are less important than in Australia because distances on any one island are relatively short.

Other Transportation

Urban centers in Australia, New Zealand, and other large islands of the South Pacific are much like those anywhere else in the world. Taxis, buses, trucks, and cars create traffic jams in Sydney, Australia, just as they do in San Francisco, California.

Many South Pacific islanders live in small villages, however. For these people, feet are the primary means of transportation on land.

Australian "cowboys"—ranchers who live in the Australian outback on huge cattle stations—may use helicopters and motorcycles at roundup time to cover the great distances their herds roam.

The Cities of Australia and New Zealand

As you can see from the map on page 36, most of the capitals and major cities of Australia and the South Pacific islands are coastal cities. This reflects the importance of the sea in the history of the region. The early explorers and settlers came by sea, and for long periods in the region's history, travel and trade was confined to boats.

As you look at individual city maps, notice the regular grid pattern of the streets—a European custom—and the many parks. Australians and New Zealanders enjoy the open green space and the opportunities for outdoor recreation that parks offer.

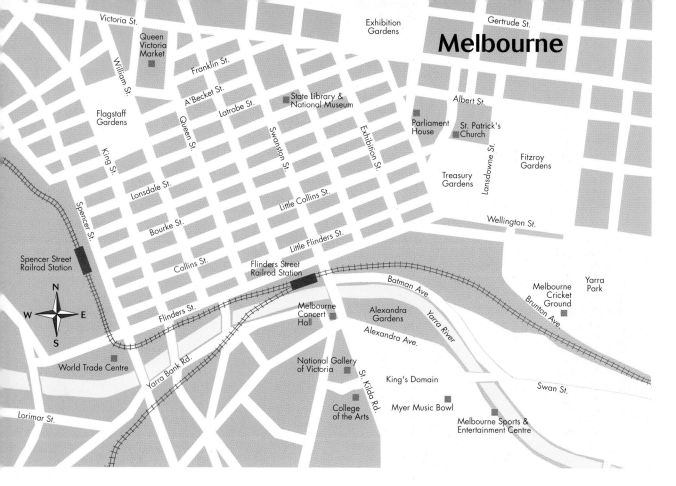

Melbourne

Melbourne

(Map labels)

Victoria St.
Queen Victoria Market
Franklin St.
A'Becket St.
Latrobe St.
William St.
Flagstaff Gardens
Queen St.
King St.
Lonsdale St.
Spencer St.
Bourke St.
Collins St.
Flinders St.
Spencer Street Railrod Station
World Trade Centre
Lorimar St.
Yarra Bank Rd.
Swanston St.
State Library & National Museum
Little Collins St.
Little Flinders St.
Flinders Street Railrod Station
Little Flinders St.
Melbourne Concert Hall
National Gallery of Victoria
College of the Arts
Exhibition St.
Exhibition Gardens
Gertrude St.
Albert St.
Parliament House
St. Patrick's Church
Treasury Gardens
Lansdowne St.
Fitzroy Gardens
Wellington St.
Batman Ave.
Alexandra Gardens
Alexandra Ave.
St. Kilda Rd.
King's Domain
Myer Music Bowl
Melbourne Sports & Entertainment Centre
Yarra River
Swan St.
Brunton Ave.
Melbourne Cricket Ground
Yarra Park

N
W   E
S

▼ *Below: The Yarra River cuts through downtown Melbourne.*

Melbourne

Melbourne is Australia's second-largest city and the capital of the state of Victoria. The city also served as the nation's capital until it was replaced by Canberra in 1927. Parliament House, located east of the central city, now houses Victoria's governmental bodies. St. Patrick's church, to the east, offers a landmark at night, when its spires are lit by floodlights.

Sports are an important part of life in Melbourne. They include everything from rowing on the Yarra River to watching Australian-Rules football and cricket matches at the Melbourne Cricket Ground. You'll find the river running across the bottom of the map. The Cricket Ground, in Yarra Park (on the eastern side of the map), was built as the main stadium for the 1956 Olympic Games.

Among Melbourne's museums are the National Gallery of Victoria and the State Library and Museum of Victoria. The National Gallery, southeast of Flinders Street Railroad Station, is noted for its art collection and the stained-glass ceiling in its Great Hall. The Gallery, and Melbourne Concert Hall to the north, are part of the Victorian Arts Centre—the cultural center of Melbourne. Ballet, opera, and orchestral performances take place there.

The State Library and Museum of Victoria, located west of Parliament House, was built in 1853 during Victoria's gold rush. At the library you can find the records from the Robert Burke and William Wills expedition of 1860–1861—the first north-south crossing of Australia. The museum features natural history, science, and technology exhibits. Queen Victoria Market, in the northwest section of Melbourne's downtown, is a covered marketplace built in the late 1800s on the site of the city's first graveyard.

Auckland

Auckland was founded in 1840 as New Zealand's capital, but the government offices were moved to Wellington in 1865. Auckland is still the largest city, however, and a major tourist center and port, as the transportation map indicates. The number of parks shown on the Auckland map reflects the importance of open space to urban New Zealanders. If this map were drawn to a smaller scale, to show more area, you would see even more parkland. Albert Park was built on the site of a military post that protected settlers from the Maori during the 1840s and 1850s. Remnants of the garrison's walls can still be found in the park, along with fountains, statues, and gardens. The Auckland City Art Gallery, in the southwest corner of the park, is New Zealand's oldest and largest art gallery.

▼ *Below: A glass skyscraper dominates this street scene in downtown Auckland.*

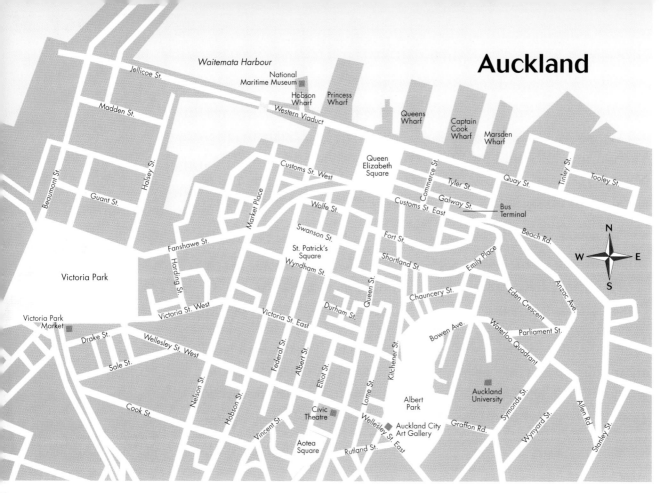

Auckland

Waitemata Harbour

Jellicoe St.
Madden St.
National Maritime Museum
Hobson Wharf
Princess Wharf
Western Viaduct
Queens Wharf
Captain Cook Wharf
Marsden Wharf

Beaumont St.
Guant St.
Halsey St.
Customs St. West
Market Place
Queen Elizabeth Square
Commerce St.
Tyler St.
Galway St.
Quay St.
Tinley St.
Tooley St.

Wolfe St.
Customs St. East
Bus Terminal
Beach Rd.

Fanshawe St.
Harding St.
Swanson St.
St. Patrick's Square
Wyndham St.
Fort St.
Shortland St.
Emily Place
Anzac Ave.

Victoria Park
Queen St.
Chauncery St.
Eden Crescent
Parliament St.
Waterloo Quadrant

Victoria Park Market
Victoria St. West
Victoria St. East
Durham St.
Bowen Ave.

Drake St.
Wellesley St. West
Federal St.
Albert St.
Elliot St.
Kitchener St.
Lorne St.
Albert Park
Auckland University
Symonds St.

Sale St.
Nelson St.
Hobson St.
Civic Theatre
Wellesley St. East
Auckland City Art Gallery
Graffon Rd.
Wynyard St.
Allen Rd.

Cook St.
Vincent St.
Aotea Square
Rutland St.
Stanley St.

Look to the west and you'll see Aotea Square. During the spring and summer, outdoor music and dance performances are held there. Aotea Centre, located in the square, is the site of indoor symphony and opera performances. Farther west, on the south side of Victoria Park, you'll find Auckland's main market bazaar.

If you follow the map north and east, you'll discover the National Maritime Museum, on Hobson Wharf at the harbor. The museum covers a thousand years of New Zealand's boating history—from Polynesian outrigger canoes to today's yachts.

Sydney

Sydney is Australia's first European settlement and its largest city. It is also the capital of New South Wales. The city began in a small area on the harbor known as the Rocks, in the northwest section of the map. On the peninsula across from the Rocks is the most famous landmark in the city—the Sydney Opera House. It is a strikingly

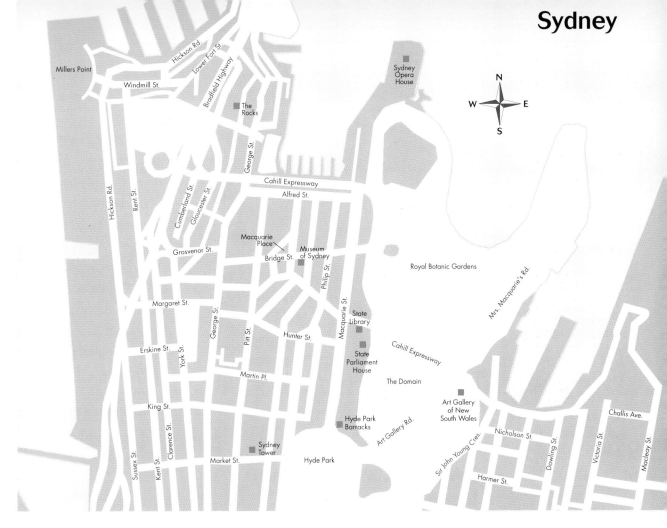

Sydney

Millers Point
Hickson Rd.
Lower Fort St.
Windmill St.
Bradfield Highway
The Rocks
George St.
Hickson Rd.
Rent St.
Cumberland St.
Gloucester St.
Cahill Expressway
Alfred St.
Sydney Opera House
Grosvenor St.
Macquarie Place
Bridge St.
Museum of Sydney
Philip St.
Royal Botanic Gardens
Margaret St.
George St.
Pitt St.
Macquarie St.
Hunter St.
State Library
Mrs. Macquarie's Rd.
Erskine St.
York St.
State Parliament House
Cahill Expressway
King St.
Martin Pl.
The Domain
Clarence St.
Sussex St.
Kent St.
Market St.
Sydney Tower
Hyde Park Barracks
Hyde Park
Art Gallery Rd.
Art Gallery of New South Wales
Sir John Young Cres.
Nicholson St.
Harmer St.
Challis Ave.
Dowling St.
Victoria St.
Macleay St.

modern building with roofs that look like billowing sails. Not as well known, but also a landmark, is Sydney Tower. This 1,000-foot (305-meter) tower, to the west of Hyde Park, is the tallest public building in Australia.

Several buildings in Sydney date from the city's beginning as a prison colony, including the State Parliament House, which was a government building, and the Hyde Park Barracks, which housed male convicts and is now a museum. Both of these structures are north of Hyde Park. In the nearby State Library, north of the Parliament House,

▼ **Below:** *The Sydney Opera House is an architectural landmark.*

1

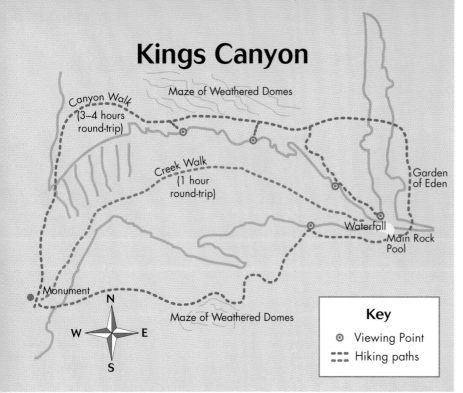

Kings Canyon

Canyon Walk
(3–4 hours
round-trip)

Maze of Weathered Domes

Creek Walk
(1 hour
round-trip)

Garden
of Eden

Waterfall

Main Rock
Pool

Monument

N

W   E

S

Maze of Weathered Domes

Key

⊙ Viewing Point

::: Hiking paths

▲ *Above: This large-scale map is designed for people on foot.*

is a copy of an early map of Australia, made by Abel Tasman in the 1600s.

Northeast of the park is another open space called the Domain. At the Art Gallery of New South Wales, located in the eastern half, are works by Aboriginal and Australian artists.

Small Macquarie Place, west of the Royal Botanic Gardens, contains various monuments relating to Sydney's early days. Nearby is the Museum of Sydney, with exhibits of the city's Aboriginal and convict history.

Other Maps and Guides

In addition to road and city street maps, there are many other maps and guides that are useful to us in moving through our world. There are navigational charts for boaters, and maps that show special points of interest, such as all the caves in a state or all the parks or monuments in a city. Floor plans that guide you through famous buildings and museums are another kind of map. And, there are trail guides for hikers, bikers, skiers, and horseback riders.

However you choose to get around our vast and complicated world—and wherever you choose to go—you will always find that maps will help you do it much more easily.

Kings Canyon

The small-scale map of Kings Canyon is designed specifically to help tourists explore this spectacular gorge on foot. The main hiking paths are indicated, as well as the time it will take for each walk. In addition, the map shows the location of scenic viewing points and major features, such as rock formations called a "maze of weathered domes," the waterfall, and rock pool. Cities with special historic districts often provide visitors with similar walking maps.

The Great Barrier Reef

As mentioned earlier, Australia's Great Barrier Reef is the largest coral reef system in the world, and it has an abundance of marine life. Scuba divers and snorkelers come from all over the world to view the reef's underwater beauty. Hundreds of islands of all sizes are found along the reef line. Some are small, and so flat that they are visible only at low tide. Others are large enough to support resorts. The Great Barrier Reef stretches across more than 1,200 miles (1,931 kilometers). A simplified, small-scale map such as the one above allows you to get your bearings—to locate parts of the reef in relation to the mainland and get an overall sense of the reef's size. It does not represent the entire reef. A more detailed destination map—such as the one of Kings Canyon—would have to be either much larger, or take up several pages.

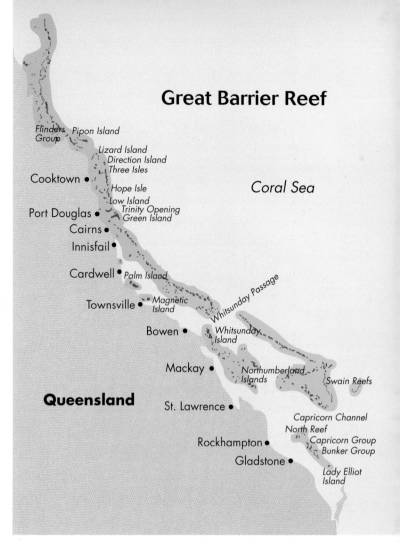

Great Barrier Reef

▲ *Above: This map includes most of the Great Barrier Reef, which extends north to Papua New Guinea.*

A Closer Look

Imagine that you've taken a trip to Australia and decided to visit Kings Canyon. Which walk would you take to see the waterfall? When a map shows "viewing points," these are usually great spots to take pictures. Does the north rim or the south rim of the canyon have the most picture possibilities?

Glossary

Aborigine Original native inhabitant of Australia.

atoll An island, or group of islands, that combines with a reef to encircle a shallow body of water called a "lagoon."

colonization Occupying another country to make use of its resources.

deforestation Large-scale clearing of forested land, which may die as a result.

desertification The creation of desert conditions caused by long droughts, overgrazing, or soil erosion.

drought A long period without rainfall.

export Something sold and shipped to another country.

gorge A deep valley with high, rocky sides.

gross domestic product (GDP) The total output of a country; all products and labor.

hardwood Broadleaf trees (see **softwood**).

indigenous Original to a particular place.

isthmus A narrow strip of land connecting two large land masses.

marsupials Animals that carry their young in pouches.

monolith A huge stone; can be many miles around and hundreds of feet high.

outback The isolated interior of Australia, or of another country.

per capita Per person (literally, "per head").

plateau A large, mostly level, area of land that is higher than the land surrounding it.

salinization The process by which nutrients are washed from the soil by over-irrigation, leaving the soil encrusted with salts.

softwood Coniferous, or cone-bearing, trees.

stations Large Australian sheep and cattle ranches.

strait A narrow body of water that connects two larger bodies of water.

subsistence farming Growing crops or raising animals for personal use, rather than for sale or trade.

Further Reading

Allison, Robert J. *Australia*. Country Fact Files (series). Austin, TX: Raintree Steck-Vaughan, 1996.

Asia, Australia, New Zealand, Oceania. Vol. 1 of Lands and Peoples (series). Danbury, CT: Grolier, Inc., 1997.

Australia . . . in Pictures. Minneapolis, MN: Lerner Publications Company, 1990.

Darian-Smith, Kate. *Exploration into Australia*. Parsippany, NJ: New Discovery Books, 1996.

Darian-Smith, Kate and Lowe, David. *The Australian Outback and Its People*. New York: Thompson Learning, 1995.

Fox, Mary Virginia. *New Zealand*. Chicago: Childrens Press, 1991.

——————. *Papua New Guinea*. Enchantment of the World (series). Chicago: Childrens Press, 1994.

Meisel, Jacqueline Drobis. *Australia: The Land Down Under*. Exploring Cultures of the World (series). Tarrytown, NY: Marshall Cavendish, 1997.

New Zealand . . . in Pictures. Minneapolis, MN: Lerner Publications Company, 1990.

Rajendra, Vijeya and Sundran Rajendra. *Australia*. Exploring Cultures (series). Tarrytown, NY: Marshall Cavendish, 1991.

Stark, Al. *Australia: A Lucky Land*. Parsippany, NJ: Dillon Press, 1997.

Index